An

with warmest best wishes

THE FIELD NEXT TO LOVE

MARILYN GEAR PILLING

Oct 4/05

*"She was blood, she was kin, she was above all
familiar, and in me, familiar occupies the field
next to love; there are places along the border
where I cannot tell one from the other."*

National Library of Canada Cataloguing in Publication

Pilling, Marilyn Gear, 1945-
       The field next to love / Marilyn Gear Pilling.

Poems.
ISBN 0-88753-364-7

       I. Title.

PS8581.I365F53 2002   C811'.54   C2002-903040-4
PR9199.3.P4965F44 2002

The Palm Poets Series is published by Black Moss Press at
2450 Byng Road, Windsor, Ontario N8W 3E8. Black Moss
books are distributed in Canada and the U.S. by Firefly Books,
3680 Victoria Park Ave., Willowdale, Ont. Canada. All orders
should be directed there.

Black Moss would like to acknowledge the generous support
of the Canada Council and the Ontario Arts Council for its
publishing program.

Le Conseil des Arts | The Canada Council
       du Canada | for the Arts

ONTARIO ARTS COUNCIL
CONSEIL DES ARTS DE L'ONTARIO

This book is dedicated to

my parents, Jean and John Gear, 1918-1999

and to T.W. McKergow

Acknowledgements

My heartfelt gratitude and special thanks: to everyone at Black Moss and especially Marty Gervais; to TM, who took seriously the first poem I ever wrote; to Don Coles who, though I was a stranger, freely offered editing and comment in the early days; to John Ferns who welcomed me as if I were family to my first Hamilton Poetry Centre workshop, and provided sustained and intelligent encouragement for my early efforts; to J. S. Porter, longtime companion in the father fields, who made a poet of me: encouraging, inspiring, cajoling, demanding, feeding me poet after poet from his library, writing critiques of my work, never giving up or letting go; to John B. Lee, whose work has always inspired me, who edited the final version of this manuscript and provided crucial help in placing it; to the members of the poetry group of the mid nineties, each of whom influenced the formation of these poems: Eugene Combs, Linda Frank, Rosalind Grant, Alphonse Lanza, Alvaro Tortora, Duane Williams; to the members of the little workshop of today, whose support, companionship, and critiques are crucial: Linda Frank, Bernadette Rule, John Terpstra; to the attendees of the Hamilton Poetry Workshop, too numerous to mention by name, whose suggestions over the years have been more important than they know; to Linda Frank and Rosalind J Grant, who ordered and arranged this manuscript, forming a disparate collection of poems into a book, and whose friendship and passion for literature have deepened and enlivened my life for the past decade; to my sister Marie Gear and my husband Dan Pilling, first and last readers, lifelong companions for better, for worse, without whom no book.

Once You Wrote Me A Poem About Raking Leaves

From time to time a miracle happens
just before death.
The dying one opens her eyes,
smiles at the circle of loved ones,
speaks into ears that wait
like cupped hands for last words.
Flares like a leaf in late fall.
Doctors call it the transfiguration.

> tomorrow
> is the day
> the dead
> hold sway
> when the veil
> is thinnest
> between this world
> and the other

Over coffee this morning you speak
of your son,
how he has your wife's life force,
how the running feet of his poems
trip over themselves.

Your eyes dark amber, you speak
of your daughter, her studies, her singing.
In the poem you wrote once,
you raked leaves with your son.

> tomorrow I will
> sharpen a long
> knife, draw a face
> on a plump vegetable
> gouge eyes
> from orange flesh
> pull seeds
> from cold slime

6

After coffee you walk me home
through beauty's zenith
beneath trees of cadent yellow,
drifting, desultory leaves.
Under transfigured trees
the squirrels are a chittering
of busy mouths; they bulge
with secret hiding places.
Though it is morning, the blue
haze of sky has a twilight feel,
the columns of slanting light
occasionally guttering.

        tomorrow night
        tiny gypsies
        will come
        to my door
        their fathers
        will hang
        back, shadows
        under the fir tree

Missing as we walk
through shifting tints of amber light
is the scent of the autumns
of my childhood, yours too, no doubt:
burning leaves. Smoldering piles
every little way, burning
like the ghats of Varanasi,
drifts of smoke the deceptive twist
of the thinning veil.

        tomorrow night
        big boys
        will come to my door
        pillowcase bags
        open wide, the wine
        god entering
        through the breaks
        in their voices

As we walk, I daydream of throwing
our papers high, watching them dally,
drift down, flutter higher.
I want to play Frisbee with our books,
throw them till their spines wobble
and they come unbound and lose their jackets,
like Peter Rabbit. I want to go rake
a big pile of leaves,
run and jump and play in them.

    tomorrow
    a squirrel
    will bark
    at the cat
    jack o'lanterns
    will leer from porches
    the dead
    will be watching

I want us to lie buried beneath
the leaves, gnarled roots
at our back, scent of maple,
withered tubers, mouldering decay.
I want us to jump out, scare
a passerby. In the poem you
wrote about raking leaves

with your son, you asked
what I would do with leaves.

    tomorrow
    the dead
    will come close
    I will open
    my door
    to masked supplicants
    will welcome
    the stranger

With a body of words
I have kissed you; you say
those are the best kind of kisses.
One day, when we are
old and full of days ourselves,
I will rake you a tall pile of them.
Tenderly I will help you down
among them, take your outstretched
hand and join you there.
On our backs, we will kick
them high, all those years of
discarnate kisses, carmine
flares against our last sky.

9

The Field Next To Love

The Field Next To Love

My Aunt was fat. She wore her moustache gladly
to church. I am pie-deprived. I pursue my
moustache relentlessly. Admire iconoclasts.

My Aunt sang hymns with a voice like grass held
between your thumbs and blown on. Her God her Master,
submitted to with fervour. My God's in hiding.

My Aunt said hoity toity and by golly. She'd been
wedlocked sixty years when she died. I know the
meaning of icthyophagous. I've been divorced.

My Aunt wiped hendirt off warm eggs as she
listened in on the party line. I flame my enemies
electronically, send blind copies indiscriminately.

My Aunt and I had nothing in common, yet
I loved her. She was blood, she was kin,
she was above all

familiar, and in me, familiar occupies the field
next to love; there are places along the border
where I cannot tell one from the other.

13

Journey

Down the path worn smooth by their feet
and the feet of the cattle
they come, every evening, these children
brother and sister, through the valley
across the log that spans
the creek, they walk the line between day
and night, the cattle dark
shapes against last light
scatter of grasshoppers, tremolo of
crickets, vibrato honk of a frog
just as they cross the log bridge,
jerk of water striders
on the surface below
flavour of creek, black muck
and wild mint, rail fence
slippery wet against bare legs.

14

Up the lane to the barn, they run
to meet buns of horse and pats of cow
straw, old stone and large warm beasts.
In the stable, corners and beams
hung with nests of swifts and spiders' silk
their Uncle's grip on the teat creates
a hard steady ping of milk on pail,
like a heartbeat or the hypnotic clop
of a horse's hooves.

Later on they emerge with the sealer
curved and warm, the milk, washed blue
of the saltlick, these two,
down the lane, over the fence,
across the log, up the path
now dark, to home.

Outhouse

babies are sometimes born
with gills, or tails, but this
is hushed up, just as

our mother wallpapered
the outhouse, silver suns
among golden stars

sent us together each day
after breakfast
my brother and I

down the path through the pines
to purge our inner
labyrinths

there were two holes

we fought for the smaller
fearing the larger, fearing
to lose our grip

16

on the worn grey seat
and slip
from this world

the wide open door
had fused with the earth,
from our perch on the holes

we watched the wind
in clover and bellflower
celandine and cinquefoil

within, borborygmus,
fat fly buzzings

beyond, cow's-belly-curve
of the horizon

below, the feral pull
of that world

17

Will Bull

On a short chain in the first stall
stood Will. We sidled past,
brushed against rough,
cool, cobwebbed stone
well away from his hooves.
His head turned sideways, one red eye
burned the cool gloom of the morning
stable, then a sudden sharp yank
on the chain by his urgent neck
sent us flying by. We knew Will was
father to every calf, husband
to every cow, this the cause of his
blue-murder intentions.

18

When Will was out, we crossed
fields the long way, never far
from the fence, not fooled
by the droning afternoon, the harmless
sun, the dawdle of small, white, butter-
flies. Within leap of the fence
we crossed fields hoping
for the glitter of Will's magic stick,
to dash straight across risked
ram trample gore.
                    Beneath us
ran faultlines; a heave or a throw,
and the earth could split open;
in those fields, the common sowthistle,
the most homely ragwort
trembled in the anticipation of a god.

19

Eight

She leans her belly against the hot thumping body
of the wringer washer, pleased that even her
useless dead-end finger of an appendix is getting
all shook up. Her mother is telling stories
of children who were not careful. Children whose
hand and arm went through the wringer.

She wants to know more. Why did they let their
fingers get too close, were their hands flat forever,
did it feel like getting born, was the ambulance pulled
by a horse like the milkman's cart used to be,
would the ambulance be delayed by the horse
arching its tail to release hot buns so strong
your nose hairs lay down and died?
Her mother does not know.

The black cylinders of the wringer roll towards
one another. With a smooth stick, she fishes
in the dirty rinse water, pulls up a bulging pair
of jeans, a ballooning checked shirt. She feeds
them to the wringer. Reamed, they stream
giant tears, emerge as flat stork shapes.

To feed the socks, her fingers must edge closer
to the ceaselessly moving cylinders, and now
she sees that it may not have been carelessness.
She flops wet socks at the wringer, pushes them
up to the moving crack, fishes and feeds,
fishes and feeds, edges ever closer to
transformation.

21

Among Shoes

In the hiatus between Christmas
turkey and pudding, I slide quietly
under the table to lie among shoes,
their friendly scuffed faces,
their homely smells of leather
and private sweating, their
harboured rows of invisible squished toes,
their diffident shuffling to accommodate
the stranger now among them,
her expanses of awkward flesh,
her long white limbs of no discernible use,
her alien smell. As I wiggle myself
into fetal position for a nap, nose
next to my aunt's swollen ankle,
knees flush with my uncle's
shining smiling polished toes, I am
suddenly at peace, have come home,
have found my place among shoes.

Dumb-Waiter

You are from the days
when it was unremarkable
to be blind or crippled
deaf or dumb. You went
to the cellar after each meal
with what they thought
would spoil upstairs with us
and stayed until they called you
back to the pantry, dirt floors
hard at your heels, silence
and servitude your mien.
In your day, death stretched
stark in the front room, the
earthen cellar sent draughts
of cool to sleepwalk through
the house, bats stargazed
from the attic, strayed
into dark bedrooms. Mornings
pee strengthened in white
chamber pots, autumns
flies seethed in thousands
through cracked walls.
Water waited in the well.

23

Now, those who sent you down
and called you up, sent me in
to load you and unload you,
are gone. I face your mute
honey pails and empty mason
jars alone, send you on
one last trip down. Your
voice, a susurrus first,then
the rumbling of a multitude
awakened.

24

Henhouse Longing

is the substrate of this day
identified at last
as the sun moves into the west

a yearning for
feathery kafuffles, crooning
sudden flurries, rushes
voices raised from cluck to cackle
subsiding to chittering flutter
jerking, naked, pointy rumps

If you would know stupidity
said Kant
look in the eye of a chicken.

Today I pine for that eye
sicken and die
for a place on the roost –
to hunch dumb among fowl
breathing gleams
of slanting straw dust light

Father

We traveled the road every weekend from our home in the city to the farm where you grew up. Half an hour from the city were the hills. The purple hills, you called them, for that was their colour at dusk. At the top of the first hill, you switched off the ignition. As the motor died, our mother begged you not to do it. As the car gathered speed, she covered her face with her hands.

Released from the motor, brake pedal outlawed, the car hurtled down the steep hill with escalating abandon. Your rule for yourself was that every bit of speed we gained in the descents must be available to take us over the rises between the descents and all the way up the last hill. Only the steering wheel could be used to control our flight.

You piloted us around the curve at the bottom of the first hill. The car lurched and swung; we slid heavily to the left. Our mother screamed. Next there was a slight rise in the road which slowed us only slightly, then a steep descent with a series of hilly curves at the bottom.

The car lunges at the descent, no longer a car but a wild creature we cling to. Now we have slipped the fetters of our lives – the fields of wheat and corn, the cattle and sheep and horses, the barns and long straight garden rows – all slide by like jet streams harnessed to a whippet, out there in the world we left in the instant the motor switched off and the car jerked free and anything became possible. We are up here in a funneling wind, a midway ride to parts unknown, an accelerating rush on the far edge of control. The screams of your family are siren calls luring you to ever greater daring.

On the last ascent we lose speed. As we crest the hill, you switch the key that returns us to our lives. Our mother sobs quietly in the front seat, we uncurl stiff white fingers from the door handles. Your soft-blue eyes are midnight-blue at these times, your pupils huge, your face flushed and shining wet.

Your name for it was coasting.

Cold Storage

You fed me
apples at bedtime
spy apples you picked
from ancient forked trees
apples you stored
at the Meatpackers
bushels brought one by one
from cold storage
to the home cellar

28

apples tasting of meat
cut in quarters, offered
one by one, white
on a knifepoint, white
of the eye rolled
before slaughter, red
skins gleaming, red
of the hot gush
of slaughter

apples cold with the jolt
of the electric fence
you let me touch, unwarned,
cold of your silences,
cold of the Inferno's
ninth circle, below water,
below hell fires, below mud,
bedtime apples
from you, my father

Father

my mother, looking at you, her eyes
green and brown and yellow with black specks
like the odd marble among clear marbles
in the faded bag in the toy box

your eyes chicory blue of the round pond
that held the sky at the marsh edge
of the summer farm

there was not one thing right about you

when I asked you a question she answered

I spoke to you as she did
like the serf in the history book, foot
upraised *who had nothing to kick but his dog*

the cards from colleagues at Christmas,
on your birthday, their messages, their warmth,
a surprise, inexplicable

on a summer day I went alone with you
for binder twine, the Austin in creeper
grinding straight up the gravel hill
to the top, I chipping away at you

you stopped, broke into my talk
your eyes – that flash of chicory, slipping
of minnows, ripples above an invisible
bottom. *You see me now with your mother's eyes.*
When you grow up you will see me with your own.

I looked away, the countryside
from the top of that hill unreal, toy farms
at the mercy of one sweep of your arm

my eyes, cat's eye green, bordered blue
taking fifty years to come clear

Wedding Photograph

Father breaks into fat her but
thin him describes her father better.
The picture is old. It shows her
coming down the aisle on the arm
of her thinhim. Now she sees this
picture with the eyes of the years.
Sees her hand clenched so as least
to touch her thinhim. Clenched
so only her nails long and sharp
and her sleeve with no heart will
touch him. Palm secreted from him.
Raising her has earned him this.
The years will cart it away
load by load.

She is in white. Thinhim wears a black
suit. She is veiled. Her dress is knee-
length, modest, flowers simple. The veil
is a creation, proportioned for a gown
whose train could carry all the wedding
guests. The veil's first layer hides
her face, the others form a nimbus.
As she nears the back of the man
at the altar, he will turn to face her,
thinhim will re form into father, father
will break into tears. The first
layer of the veil softens her world.
When it is lifted, she will
enter harsher time.

33

Father

On this path familiar
as the curves and mounds
of my body, this path that bends
past plump hills secret with tunnels,
among trees of thorn whose limbs are webbed,
where cornflowers tap my ankles and
blue shells of robin eggs scatter,
always I am looking for you.

34

this is the farm you called
The Other Place, here was neither
house nor barn, we were forbidden
to speak of this farm. Here
was your war. You hacked thorn trees
burned tent caterpillars, drove your car
to gopher holes, poured exhaust
down tunnels. You strung
a fence along the high banks
of the river, on my thigh is a
scar from the barbed wire.

This day, I leave the path
follow a side trail through
long grass to a pond that will be gone
by summer, in the sponge of mud at its border

hundreds of frogs the size of thimbles,
lucent golden frogs with a sticky,
delicate feel.

Are these the froggies that
never knew a story or a rhyme at all?
Will I free you if I catch them,
if I kiss them as they fly one
by one through my fingers?

Father

There were all those stories
about you
how you stood on your head
in a canoe
folded yourself into woodboxes
and waved with your feet
how you climbed the cherry tree
and packed your cheeks
round with pits
like our mother's with the mumps
how you won the wheelbarrow
and three-legged races
how you swam the river
all the way to the lake.
There were all those stories
but we never had proof
never even saw
any evidence

then one day
at the nursing home
I see your name
on the bulletin board:
John Gear –
Bean Ball Champion
of Brookhaven Lodge.

37

Father

how every weekend
you dug postholes
in the stony soil
dug all morning
in the hot sun
how at noon
your forearms were red
your shirt a wet dark blue
how you lifted the dipper
of cold well water
from the metal pail
how I averted my eyes
from your nostrils
flared as you drank
how you weren't sitting down
before I was digging
at you

how the other day
at breakfast
I raised my tall glass
of juice and drank
how my daughter
averted her eyes
placed the large box
of corn flakes
between us

how one hot day
this August
I decided to walk
the length
of the fences you fixed
count the holes you dug
how by noon I was spent
having gone less
than one third
the distance
having lost track
of the holes

Father

Pepper swarms of sparrows above white
shivery-brittle corn
goldenrod bent brown in the hollows
the transmigration of leaves.

he's taken a turn
        a little turn
for the worse

I know the place

at the west of the farm you worked
all your life
where the banks are high
and straight, the descent a slide
through roots and muck past
quagmire caves of leaf mold
to the walnut-wrinkled, dun-brown flats
of the river.

Yesterday I held you
your body like the barn board
beside the silo, stiff
in the watery sun
eyes blue in the mask
of your face

Today as I walk
the path at the top of the high banks
I glimpse you
far below by the river, see you take
the little turn
                    towards the rowboat
scraping gently in the shallows.

41

Her Last Legs

I'm on my last legs
says my mother,
she means the ones she keeps
in the drawer wrapped in tissue paper
under her clean underwear
with the lavender sachet on top,
the legs she brings out for special
occasions when the demands on her
are more than human,
for instance when our father gets
that he can't look after himself and
she can't bear to put him in the nursing home,
she brings out her last legs
and there's nothing she can't do –
they're the Last Post, the Last Rites
and the Last Ditch Stand rolled into one.
When we saw her coming on those legs,
she didn't have to open her mouth,
we picked up the toys, we went to bed,
we turned out the light.

When our mother dies,
there's only one thing I want,
I tell my sister, and that's
her last legs.
I don't know, she says, do you think
they'll stay in the drawer?
don't you think they'll still be charging around
visiting our dad, driving our uncle to church
carrying soup to the lady upstairs?
when we're old and sick ourselves
don't you think we'll hear them rustle by
to the medicine cabinet
still smelling faintly of lavender?

43

Mother

those girlhood winters,
my forehead tight with cold, third eye
frozen shut for decades

flesh that years later will burn
and redden
as life returns

till then I
grown child
returned home each weekend

to you, flew
like a robin
at the self

in the window
my self your self
bashed again and again

44

at the same
gleaming spot on the glass
bits of feathers spiraling pink

onto the lengthening grass
these words
you utter only now the bird has ceased

to fly against the glass – *I wonder*
if your coat was warm enough
those winters?

even as my daughter sets forth
wet hair already forming
into Gorgon ice

45

To My Mother On Boxing Day Evening

This is what they call an open winter, so though
it is December, the Maitland river
curls slowly downstream in secretive spirals

and we, on the brink of departure – your daughters,
son, niece and nephew – beg you for a last song,
cajole you to the piano.

You begin softly, *Flow gently*
sweet Afton among thy green braes,
flow gently I'll sing thee a song in thy praise...

like roses brought indoors to float in crystal,
our eyes drift in the bowl of their tears,
so you sway in beauty seen through water,

and we cast forth silken draglines of longing
that glint, for an instant, here and there
in the candlelight, *my Mary's asleep*

46

by thy murmuring stream, while I, your firstborn,
silently promise the impossible – to tiptoe
barefoot and blindfolded across the summer pasture

avoiding all thistles, *flow gently sweet Afton,*
disturb not her dreams, to carry a spider's web intact
from the west field to the old silo, *a place*

that's known to God alone, to lift a dandelion
into the wind without losing one parachute-borne seed.
If I complete these tasks, will we be allowed

to keep you? Our love has been a bouquet
of buttercups tangled with bristlegrass
and pokeweed, *we'll find perfect peace,*

where joys never cease, yet now
it is all of you we seek to keep – your
pokeweed as much as your oatmeal

cookies with the date fillings, your knitted
dishclothes, the old songs you play,
your cleverness at Scrabble –

it is the singularity
of you we seek to keep
out there beneath a kindly sky.

But now your tempo quickens,
you swing into *I'll be down to get you with a taxi*
honey, your frailty is slipping from your shoulders

like a silk cloak, *better be ready about*
half-past-eight, your eyes are the green
of your twenty-fifth year, there is a carefree

48

slant to your sudden smile, coquette,
you tilt your head
gonna dance out both o' my shoes

when they play them jelly roll blues, and we
lean forward to listen beyond your notes,
though we know what is out there –

at the river's near bank,
the rowboat
scraping gently in the shallows.

The Still Waters. To My Mother At Eighty

A Journey Through Open Heart Surgery

i.   the way to the hospital
passes under tall trees
passes through maple
maple my home, maple my native, maple my land
maple scent sun-warm, pervasive

scuffle of maple dust
maple pale lemon to maple deep topaz
maple slowing my tempo to shuffle
each day there is one, then another
that I must take to you

on your white coverlet
pliant, gracious petiole, questing veins
curving midrib shedding gold into scarlet
blade bleeding crimson into jagged
apex, transpiration ceased

you and I, heads bowed over maple
maple our home, maple our native, maple our land
yet maple not seen until now

49

when I raise your window
instant animation –
now they loiter on a wind puff
tap you lightly on your cheek
stun you with their hectic ruby dance

tomorrow they will break at my touch
next week   scuttle in the gutters
next summer ashes, dust

ii.   The night before the surgery
     your roommate tells you your chest
     will be split open with an ax,
     your heart set aside in a dish.

     "What sort of dish?" From the hall
     I hear you ask her that.
     "Cut glass," she says, "you know,
     the sort of dish you use
     for serving pickles. Can't you
     just see your poor old heart
     in that dish, oozing and flopping
     like a fish that can't breathe?"

"But what if it flops out
onto the floor, the floors
aren't so clean in this place."

"Oh, that happens all the time,
don't worry, they give it
a good scrub
before they sew it back in,
let me tell you, honey,
that's the least of your worries
tomorrow."

iii. These last weeks, I've longed
for one more story,
something about your life
you've never told me.
Just before sundown
they wash you all over, coat you
in a special solution and when
they have gone, you tell me

how your father was short
but his arms and chest and shoulders
were muscular, covered
with dark curly hair

how every night
when your father came in from the fields
he would wash
his arms and chest and shoulders
how the old sink in the kitchen
was deep and wide and looked out
on the pasture that sloped to the river
how your father would lather
his arms and chest and shoulders
then fill the dipper and rinse it all off
how then your mother would go to your father
and soap his back, lather it over and over
both of them looking out on the pasture
that sloped to the river

your eyes now on the setting sun
watching your mother washing your father's
back, her hand making the journey
over and over

iv   After supper the boydoctor bounds
into your room flourishing paper.
This time he wants your permission.
Again he explains the procedure,
the hoped for results, then,

like a waiter listing the specials
presents the risks –
"You can have stroke," he nods,
encouragingly,
"you can have heart attack," he bobs,
frantically,
and now his merry visage twists to sad
clown face
as he squeaks, "You can even die!"

You grab the pen and sign,
then, his footsteps still audible,
we succumb to our laughter, the laughter
of teenaged girls in church.
Always a mimic, you put on his happy face
"You can have stroke," you parrot,
nodding up at me.
"You can have hut attuk,"
you mimic, cruelly,
as I jump to my feet and grandly
shriek, "You can even **die!**"

When I begin to recover,
you set me off again with your
mimic's face, your story of the sandwich

the technician found beneath a woman's breast
a sandwich cuddled up to the heart,
and so our laughter
carries us helpless through the evening,
sweeps us surely to the juncture
where I cannot follow,
though this night has been
the time in all my life
when I've least wanted
to part from you.

54

v.   In 1969, we were heading west,
driving from Ontario to Manitoba.
As we approached Thunder Bay,
Neil Armstrong neared the moon.
We dropped into the lobby of a small hotel
to watch him step onto the moon's surface
in fuzzy black and white.
All the way there, the speculation -
what would his first words be,
this first of our kind
to step onto the moon?

Just so we wonder, my sister and I,
what our last words to you will be,
your last words to us.

"Will you prepare?" asks my sister.

"No, Neil Armstrong prepared, and disappointed
the world."

At the end of the evening, we hug you hard.
"Bye Mom," we croak.

You blow a kiss and pirouette on swollen legs
like Pierre Trudeau behind the Queen.

vi.   it has been seen so often on TV
      that it is familiar
      the machines surrounding each bed, tubes, monitors, IV's,
      a nurse for every patient

> *machines hiss, bellow, pump*
> *tubes carry fluid to and from*
> *there is no day or night here*
> *endless artificial light*

we walk the length
scrub at the sink
approach your bed

and there, bare shouldered, toga'd in white like a citizen
of ancient Rome, you lie, so like your mother
in her coffin, the machine breathing in, breathing out
with surprising force

hiss, bellow, machines pump
fluid to and from tubes carry
day or night there is no here
artificial endless light

she looks good
her numbers are good
says your nurse

56

in the vise of that determined machine, you look as if
you have been to a far country
you look so ravaged, so ancient, so white, such a long, long
way from coming back to life

bellow pump, hiss, machines
carry from fluid tubes to and
is there no here night or day
light artificial endless

vii. He comes to us in the quiet room to tell us
your heart has stopped again, has again
been shocked to life, if it happens a third time

should they let you go? A question to ponder
along with our supper. "Your mother is eighty,"
he says, on his way out the door.

Yes, you are eighty, and I am fifty, and he looks
thirty, and my daughter is twenty, and a cow
has four stomachs, a cat has nine lives, there are

ninety-nine bottles of beer on the wall, countless
fish in the sea, the clock struck one
the mouse ran down, I run after

catch up to him,
turn him, tell him:
"our mother is Our Mother."

viii. later that night
the quiet room is not quiet
the walls stream tears
sofa, chairs, pillows
bob in salt water, sodden

they bump against walls and
upended tables, slowly they
sink and we are going down
with them, going under, as
in this streaming unquiet
we write your
obituary

there on the floor going glug
ears filling with water
open eyes smarting,
there, heavier than salt
water, we wrestle your life
into a shape
we cannot agree on,
your son wants no mention of his
newly-divorced wife
your daughter insists she be
mentioned, I swim between
them, going glug

when we have finished
we float to the surface, bellies up

your life there beside us, so little
a paragraph holds it entire

a doctor comes to the door
pulls the plug

tells us
you will live

ix. Back on the ward at last
you do not seem like my mother.
You have a strange new whimper
a strange new way of rocking
yourself, you are somebody's dolly
crying for comfort no one
can give, not I, not the nurses
not my sister, my brother.
Coming in, one day, I hear you
from far down the hall, you are
nobody's dolly now, the sound
you make is strange
yet familiar, an ageless cry
that has battered itself
on the hardest stone, the most arid
land, a sound edged and shot through
with an ancient sorrow, it is a
keening I hear, a lamentation
for the dead
             but who is dead?

x.   Through dark red vines on your window
I glimpse blue wells of sky. You rock
and you whimper, you gag on your pills,
your face a dry place of wandering
lines, blowing sand,
and then without warning, you turn
and look into my eyes
as you have not looked since strangers
looked into your heart:

     "I nearly passed over, didn't I."

60

These eyes will have truth.

     "Yes, Mom, you did."

With these words we cross a divide,
On your face for this moment
a light so radiant
it obliterates the desert
as you describe
the music, the light, the loving presence

your words so talk-show common, yet

in the light that shines from your face
I am transparent
I am sore afraid.

xi. Now we have a new mother
no longer dizzy and breathless
no longer tired, no longer dying,
you sit on your porch in a snowstorm
you let the heat in your living room
rise to one hundred degrees,
you eat ten oranges for dinner
wear the same clothes every day
sleep in a chair, wear a towel
around your neck, like a trainer,
you'd wear the towel to church
if we let you. Evenings
you sit silent, on your face
the stubborn, inward gaze
of the class dullard
confronted by fractions.
When we ask for jam you say "no,
it's for me." Friday, you phone
the hairdresser, ask her to come,
when she says she'll come
Tuesday, you say, "no,
it has to be today."

When you visit your husband
in the nursing home, you force
ginger ale down his throat,
you make him choke. When
someone asks about your scar,
you lift your skirt to your waist.
We know what to do with a new
baby, we know what to do
with a new house, a new job,
we're not sure yet
what to do with a new
mother.

xii. was it our desire that drove you through the
autumn countryside to the hospital in the big city
that afternoon

not the ambulance, but our desire that unfolded
to your eyes so long confined that impossible burning
tapestry of trees

for years you said you would not go, never would you
get up on that table, never let your heart be opened
to the eyes of strangers

so when it came to the day when the waters rose
in your lungs, was it our desire that drove you
to leave your home

to leave the slow, familiar cadence of your dying
for a hurtle through the screaming countryside
towards that table

our desire
to keep you

our inability
to open our hands
to let you go

to let you go
into the rising waters

to let you return
to the waters

the waters

the still waters

xiii *"Welcome the stranger, we are told in so many tales."*

We took you on a
journey to foil Death.

We have been given back
a stranger,
a person who looks like you,
lives at your address
knows our names and
some of your stories
yet is a stranger.

She has been given
into our keeping.
Wherever you are,
my mother,
fear not for her.
We will get to know
her, we will keep her.

Coda

i.   my sister was sleepless
and in her hand
was a tenderness beyond what was there
when I touched you, that yearning
smoothing of hair at your temples,
that gentle grace note she placed on your lips,
a tenderness that pulled
at the deepest tears
I held
     and then she looked at me and whispered

"inconceivable -
       to lose her"

her eyes the eyes of a mother bereft
        only then
did the mystery open its heart to me

My sister is childless. You were her child.

her anguish at last a place I could enter,
leave her no longer alone

ii.   You, my sister, would know the name
       of the two bones in a woman's neck
       that end before they touch, creating
       a hollow where the heart beats.
       Below there is where you cut me
       with your scalpel, excised the piece of alien
       flesh, bent over me, sewing, your eyes
       bright like our mother's,
       your lips unpainted and held in her
       it's all in the way you hold your mouth
       position, the two of you
       always so good with your hands.
       How hard you tried to save her failing heart.

       Since her death two years ago
       you have shrunk, you have become tiny and
       white-haired and you wear that little smile
       she wore to the store. You had eyes only
       for your sewing the morning you cut me,
       you did not see me watching our mother
       tenderly stitch my flesh together,
       her neat black crisscrossed lines,
       how they left on my chest your mark
       halfway between heartbeat hollow and my heart.

Woman to the Woods Singing

After Watching Red, White and Blue

Every evening of that week I watched a film
set in France
and by the end of the week I wanted to take up
smoking.
All the women smoked.
All had long legs, chic haircuts, smart shoes, purses
of soft leather that swung from one
shoulder, purses that held the knowledge
of what it was to be Woman, the props
for a life where sex filled
all the interstices.
With eyes that burned I watched
how those women opened
their purses, felt
for the package, tapped
the cigarette from its place in the row
of identical brothers.
I watched the curve
of their wrists as they flicked
on fire, quick dip
of their heads as tip touched flame.

Concentration of the first inhalation.
How then the burdens of their foreheads, necks, and
shoulders loosen and roll away,
how with the second in-breath their eyes go un-
seeing, and they curl themselves
for reverie.
Those women.
I want their legs, their haircuts, their sex lives, the secrets
of their purses, but mostly I want
those islands in their lives
where the smoke drifts effortlessly beyond their fingers and
out of time.

70

Falling

for TM

Like Alice I was looking at daisies when you walked
by it was high summer the sky a wide pure blue
deep in sweet clover and stasis I was
idly picking petals from a daisy
he loves me he loves me not he loves me
and when I glanced up more out of chance
than anything else you looked back
and I dropped my petals and followed
never expecting when you disappeared ahead
in the swaying tangle of timothy
to lose my balance just where you vanished
and fall head first down what seemed a deep crack
in the earth pleasantly cool at first
with handholds and footholds
a rope ladder that swung gently in the gloom

71

Once the moon was in the crescent of sky
I was falling away from the falling became
flying seemed like freedom seemed like swinging off
a trapeze head first towards your waiting hands
until one day when my legs let go your hands
were not there I was falling in earnest the walls
themselves shifting then disappearing
the seasons changing not knowing if deeper still
your hands would be waiting
or whether I'd ever find my way back
to the world I left with less thought than I'd give
to picking petals from a daisy
he loves me he loves me not he loves me
or flowers for the vase
pomegranate for folly
vervain for enchantment
honeysuckle for bonds of love

You Are The Woman

"You are the woman who pours the expensive jar of per-
fume
over the head of Christ. Not a portion of it, but all of it.

Every last drop." This is how you praise me, and I stare
at the woman your words evoke, for I know her.

She is my sister, whom you have never met. *In a family
one sister may conceal another,* warns the poem.

Yes, it is my sister who comes up the path, smiling,
her hair a glitter of gemlike strands, in her hands

the box of white, translucent alabaster.
She is the one who bends to enter the door

of the house of Simon the leper,
she who takes his hand in both of hers, brushes

the stump of a finger with her lips, turns
and kneels before Christ. It is my sister who stands

with sudden passion, dashes the precious box
against a stone, she who releases the perfumes of Araby

wherever she walks. I am the one who waits
in the darkest corner, I am the one who watches

as arms raised, head thrown back, she lets the priceless
perfume rain upon Christ's head and on the head

of Simon, lets it pour down her upraised arms and
pool between her breasts. I am the one who watches

74

the golden rain pick up the light, blur and meld
the edges of all three in its anointing flow;

I am the one who breathes in the scent.
In a family one sister may conceal another,

So, when you are courting, it's best to have them all in view
*Otherwise in coming to find one you may love another.**

** Italicized words are from Kenneth Koch's poem
"One Train May Hide Another"*

This Spring

This spring, I listen for you
at the threshold, listen long,
I do not hear you coming. Turning,

I find myself within, where
it is raining. My rain is gentle
at first, a mere pittering

on tender leaves, my wind a sigh,
and from the south. Beyond the threshold,
the white magnolia, meant to be

ephemeral, meant to be exquisite
for six days in spring,
endures for weeks, each blossom

a chalice brimming with water. Within,
my tulips gather each day's rain, at dusk
their cups run over.

In my darkness, fragrances arise, scent
of loosening soil and life
unfurling. In my darkness waits

the spirit of a white magnolia,
not one blossom dropping.
You do not come,

my rain falls harder, my fields are lakes
of ruffled sky, my puddles rippled mirrors,
at every grate my underground river rushes.

This spring, the white magnolia,
meant to be ephemeral, is suppliant,
a candelabra holding rain

not fire.

My Long Winter Coat

I gave you my long winter
coat to carry while I
did an errand in the opposite
direction. You took it
from me, held it with both arms
as one would hold a lady
who had fainted, fainted
because you had cursed her,
or smoked, or looked at her
a certain way. The arms
of the lady hung empty,
helpless without hands,
her furred hood flopped back
as if her neck had surrendered.
Or perhaps it was broken.
You had wrung it in a rage.
The lady dead, newly dead,
not yet stiff. You strode away,
she lay limp in your arms,
perhaps you intended to bury her.

At the corner I looked back,
saw you bow your head
bend into her hood
saw your lips
disappear
into fur.

Divide The World

for JSP

Divide the world

into those who tiptoe into
the hallowed chapel
of the book, wearing gloves

and those who roll
in the written word
as a pig rolls
in the slob slop
of the unmucked pen,
bits of straw stuck
to his full feedsack sides,
those who explore the book
as a pig explores
his trough, his
great, shining, snuffling snout
leaking and trembling and rooting
into the corners,

those who quit the book
as a pig who emerges
dazed from the pen,
regards the world thereafter
through the white eyelashes

of the sublime.

80

If You Know Apples

If you know apples you know
that a McIntosh bunches up
to its stem, swells so close
it nearly touches, you'd never
mistake it for a Spartan,
shaped like a bowl at its navel,
that the flesh of a Spy is
tinged amber, like leaves
after frost, that a Talman
Sweet is not sweet but
unique like an old Appal-
achian woman who is wholly
herself, when you cut apples
crosswise, you find the part
you don't eat, the star holding
seeds, a star at the heart of
all apples.

        If you know apples
you know it was October
when the snake spoke
leaves burning primary red
maple scenting each breath
exile and sin unconceived, it was
October and Eve only wanted that
crisp spray on her palate
the star in white flesh
the starfull of seeds

plump mystery in her palm.

82

He Leaves It To Her

He leaves it to her
to pull the worms from the kitchen
ceiling, so as not to affect
his karma, he leaves
it to her to stand on a chair and
nudge and coax their sticky length
onto a cloth and out the door,
these worms that, undisturbed, will spin
a dusky mesh to hide their change
to worm with wings.

Like the fat and skinny husks of
Pharoah's grain, they come each seventh year,
these moths, those she misses as worms,
come just at the border of light and dark
a viridian haze, a blur of wings
to haunt her twilight kitchen, they come
recurring dream, like Hecate's
spirits, to find no rest in death.

83

She has no Joseph
to interpret their repeated visits,

this year, on the chair, arms up, she slips
or perhaps surrenders to baser
desires, mashes their round rolled
selves to sticky paste,
consigns herself to one more turn
on the eternal round
even as he, karma
intact, evanesces into the purity
of the final light.

Return Of The Deserting
Wife After One Year

Two bumblebees slam
against the window.
Above the empty chair, peonies
hang from the pergola.
On the table a ball of twine.

I enter the garden
follow the thread
through the maze
of thyme and woodbine
to where you lie
among rose canes
impaled on thorns
bound by silverlace vine
fetid among henbane
at the end of the twine
you to whom
freedom meant
freedom from
bonds.

On your lids
in place of pennies
two flightless
silent
bees.

The Snowplough

On the first day of March, the male cardinal calls from the fir tree, the underground river is torrential at every manhole, little girls roller skate down the sidewalk. Though she knows the cardinal's song is not for her, she decides to shave her legs of their coat of winter hair. Snow slides down the roof and splats onto the ground. It is plus eleven degrees.

As she scrapes her leg, she hears one sound that does not fit. Surely it is not the plough. She goes to the window. A mammoth snowplough is pushing one rapidly diminishing strip of dirty ice along the gutter.

She hurries outside and climbs onto the picnic table in her side yard where she will be at the level of the man in the driver's cab, for she must see his face.

Will his expression be dogged, a face intent on doing-the-job, no judgement required or even allowed? Will his expression be proud, the face of a man at the helm of a powerful machine, never mind whether it's ploughing water or dropping bombs? Will his expression be sheepish? Steeped in an acute awareness of overkill? She hopes for this last.

Here it comes. Exhaust and cacophony. Flashing steel blade scraping all before - grit, odd mittens, the occasional loonie, a trickle of ice water. The plough blasts by.

There is no one in the driver's seat. No one at all.

She sits on the picnic table and hugs her legs. She wonders. Would you call this artificial intelligence? The industrial revolution run amok? Millennial monomania?

She shakes her head, for she does not know. She is not a Prime Minister or a City Father. She is not a computer. She is only a woman on a picnic table with one hairy leg and one smooth, the male cardinal calling and calling, the temperature plus eleven and rising.

Dug And Jug To The Gingerbread Man

Walking down Yonge
    she allows herself
to know
    how much
she loves breasts
    how much
the pleasure of any city walk
    is looking
at other women's breasts
    how much
she loves nipples
    outlined by cloth

She's been called
    'slack tit'
she's been called
    'thirty eight low'
turns off the light now
when she's on top –
    her breasts swing
    like a cow's teats
    from the udder

Walking down Yonge
　　　her breasts swing
right off
　　　cartwheel away
　　　　　towards Front -

　　　dug and jug to the gingerbread man

　　　　　merry-andrews
　　　　　　　　circling
　　　　　　　　　　just out of reach

90

Poem Made From July List
Of Favourite Words

Hullaballoo and Lollygagging
are being wed.
Carapace ushers.
Eschatology performs the ceremony.
Maven is the mother of the groom.
While Chiarascuro sings the solo,
Chicanery squirms and picks her nose,
Lollygagging's twin nephews
Flaccid and Tumescent snicker
in the next pew.
When Eschatology asks
if any man knows any reason why
Hullaballoo and Lollygagging
should not be wed,
Egregious jumps up and hollers
Ululation.
Carnal and Chalaza
are in the back row wearing red
whispering about Tatterdemalion
smoking in the vestibule.
Outside Chimera catches the bouquet.
Hitched to the buggy
are Doppelganger and Quotidian.
Timbrel holds the reins.

Fast Forward

Sometimes when I straighten
from the deep blue heart of a delphinium
I have been gone so long
that I have lost my place and must listen
to my life and fast forward, listen and
fast forward, until I remember
who I am and where, for when
first I straighten to awareness
of hot sun, damp earth, dragonfly, and leaves
I am the girl
picking blackberries with her mother
by the river, honey pail
a cool weight on my hip,
no, fast forward, I am the young mother
this weight my firstborn
as we roam the farm,
no, I am the woman
caught in the frantic mesh of
marriage, job, children,
no, here I am
in my sun-dazed garden,
this weight an earthen pot of flowers
 children grown, parents gone,
here I am,
this now my place
first in line before the unknowable.

Psalm

This is the light
that rolls over the rim of the world like a rogue wave.

This is the light
that pours golden into the corners, unrolls secrets curled like
scrolls in the drawers.

This is the light
that fills the clotheslines of the world with smacking sheets
and antic desires.

This is the light
that sends the fetus head first into the birth canal.

This is the light
that caroms off the heartwood door of sorrow,
rousing all within.

This is the light
that beats blankets, empties basements,
spreads a life upon a lawn.

This is the light
that fills the luminous green pastures with cavorting young.

This is the light
that sends men up ladders to clean out eavestroughs, teeter
on the ridgepoles of their lives

This is the light
that sends a woman to the woods singing –

> Dangle tin pails from my arms and tap me.
> The sap you get will set free spirit
> trapped in matter, cure baldness and
> impotence, salve the wounds between.

These poems have previously been published in the following journals and anthologies:
The Fiddlehead, The Antigonish Review, Quarry, The Literary Review of Canada, The New Quarterly, Gaspereau Review, Grain, Prairie Fire, Carousel, Windsor Review, Canadian Woman Studies, Contemporary Verse 2, Dandelion, Kairos, <u>*Vintage 98, Vintage 99,*</u> <u>*Following The Plough: Recovering The Rural*</u> selected and edited by John B. Lee, <u>*Smaller Than God*</u> edited by Paul Quenon and John B.Lee

The poems that make up *The Still Waters* sequence were short-listed for the 1999 League of Canadian Poets Chapbook Competition, the 2000 Shaunt Basmajian Chapbook Award, and the 2000 Acorn-Rukeyser Chapbook contest.

The Snowplough won *Prairie Fire's* Two-Minute Tales contest and was broadcast on CBC radio in April '98. *The Field Next To Love* and *Last Story* were honourable mentions in the League of Canadian Poets National Poetry Contests of '98 and '99. *Journey* has been chosen for broadcast on CBC radio. Several of these poems won Hamilton and Region Arts Council awards.

Contents